TABLE OF

Unless otherwise indicated, all Scripture quotations are taken from the King James Version of the Bible.
7 Laws You Must Honor To Have Uncommon Success/B-294
ISBN 10: 1-56394-420-0/B-294 · ISBN 13: 978-1563944208
Copyright © 2010 by **MIKE MURDOCK**
Publisher/Editor: Deborah Murdock Johnson
Published by The Wisdom Center · 4051 Denton Hwy. · Ft. Worth, Texas 76117
1-817-759-BOOK · 1-817-759-2665 · 1-817-759-0300
You Will Love Our Website..! WisdomOnline.com

Conversations Are The Birthplace For Seasons.

-MIKE MURDOCK

Why I Wrote This Book

Conversations Schedule Seasons.

God rules His world with His *mouth. Everything* God does...He does with words. He loved *words* so much He called Himself The Word. "In the beginning was the Word, and the Word was with God, and the Word was God," (John 1:1).

Words Are The Seeds...For Feelings.

Words Are The Seeds...For Change.

You can create any change you want with your mouth. Since God rules His world and His universe with His mouth, you can rule your world with *your mouth.* "For in many things we offend all. If any man offend not in word, the same is a perfect man, and able also to bridle the whole body," (James 3:2).

Conversations Are The Birthplace For Seasons.

This is one of the most explosive Wisdom Keys that God ever put in my heart: *Seasons Are Decided By Who You Trust.*

Always look for *Difference...*in an *Opportunity,* a *Moment,* but especially *People.*

...The *Focus* they are willing to *pursue.*

...The *Enemy* they are willing to *confront.*

...The *Weakness* they are willing to *correct.*

...The *Mentor* they are willing to *trust.*

I cannot change your life until I change the voice you *trust.* You can have breakfast every morning and travel frequently with a man of God. This will not necessarily change your life. Demas traveled with Paul, yet he was still attracted to the things of the world.

(See 2 Timothy 4:10.)

Having a great father who is articulate, perceptive, passionate and discerning does not guarantee success. Absalom and Solomon had the same father. One was a fool; the other was the wisest man who ever lived on the Earth. *I cannot change your life until I change whose voice you honor.*

Having a Mentor who knows your weakness, and is willing to endure it for you to unleash your strength and your gift, will not necessarily change your world. John, the beloved, and Judas Iscariot had the same Mentor...*Jesus. I cannot change your life until I change the Mentor you trust.*

A Brazilian pastor asked me a few weeks ago, "What do you do when God quits talking?"

I said, "I check my hearing." God is *rarely* silent. In my personal opinion, He actually *never* stops talking.

Say these words aloud: "Precious Holy Spirit, I am a passionate protégé. I will master the Art of Learning. I am listening. I will hear Your Voice. Amen."

I want to share with you 7 Laws...*7 Laws You Must Honor To Have Uncommon Success.*

There are 7 Laws you must acknowledge... embrace for you to experience Uncommon Success.

Success is the obtaining of something worthwhile.

Success is not a *Season*.

Success is not a *Place*.

Success is an Experience.

You can create Successes by the Moment...by the *day*...by the *hour.* You have already collected thousands of Successes in your life. It is important for you to see that Successes can become *habitual... continuous...consecutive.* God wants you to *enjoy*

Success.

An example of Success is Dr. Morris Cerullo, an Apostle Paul of our generation. At 78 years old, he is still going all over the world instead of sleeping in a hammock in Honolulu. He has had *uninterrupted, relentless* Successes. You can have the same kind of life.

In this book, I believe God is going to speak a word to you...relating to your Assignment on the earth...and any Problem-Zone in your life.

That is why I wrote this book.

Mike Murdock

Your Ignorance
Is The Only Weapon
Satan Possesses.

-MIKE MURDOCK

My Personal Persuasions

———————»-◎-«———————

Every Problem Is Always A Wisdom Problem.
God will never answer a prayer for which He has already given you an equation. Problems must be confronted. That is why we teach. If God was going to solve all your problems, mentorship would be unnecessary.

He is a *Teacher.*

He made us *Learners.* He is *looking* for Learners.

Sometime ago aboard an airline flight, someone asked me, "What do you do for a living?"

I smiled. "I am a Learner."

He said, "I mean, what do you do for a living?"

I said, "That is what I do. I am a Learner."

My banker asked me, "What is your hobby Dr. Murdock?"

I said, "Learning! That is what I do."

Why have I made that my Life-Focus? I have discovered so much stupid in me that I am anxious to overcome!

The *only* problem in your life is *ignorance.*

Your Ignorance Is The Only Weapon Satan Possesses. The only weapon your enemy has is your stupidity.

"My people are destroyed for lack of knowledge," (Hosea 4:6). *Ignorance* is destroying you; not a demon... not a devil. Never be afraid of a devil. Be afraid of being stupid. *'Stupid'* is different from being *ignorant.*

Ignorance is...simply not knowing.
Stupidity is...*not caring* to know.
Do you have a desire to *know?*
Do you have a desire to *learn?*
Picture scrolls, 1,000 miles long, hanging from the floor of Heaven toward the earth. Imagine every scroll is a collection of Wisdom by topic. On each scroll is a different Law and all relating knowledge to it.

The Law of Reproduction

There is a scroll on the Law of Reproduction. Everything God wants you to know on the Law of Reproduction is written on that scroll.

Whatever You Are You Reproduce.

If you are an Irishman, you reproduce Irishmen. If you are German, you reproduce Germans. If you are a tomato, you reproduce tomatoes.

The Law of Loss

Anything Unprotected Will Be Stolen.

Battle is the Seed for territorial control and ownership. Anything sent from God will require battle on your part.

The Law of Loss...Anything unprotected can be taken, because you are in an adversarial environment...with a master thief. Satan is not your normal bank burglar. He is a *master thief.*

Every Loss Is The Seed For Restoration.

A Seed for a seven-fold return is within anything satan has stolen from you.

The Law of Change

Picture a thousand mile scroll documenting all the facts about the topic of change. *Change Is Always Proportionate To Knowledge.*

Pain *never* produces change.

Pain produces *desire* for change.

Knowledge Is The Seed For Change.

The purpose of knowledge is to create change.

Time does not create change.

Need does not produce change.

Knowledge *produces* change.

Time does not teach. There are 90-year-old sinners and 15-year-old Christians. Gray hair does not make you wise. A bald head does not make you smart either!

Time does not change your wealth. There are 25-year-old millionaires and 80-year-old paupers.

Laws matter. More than Miracles...Fate...or Luck. In this book, I share with you 7 Laws that will create Uncommon Success.

The Two Parts of The Gospel

The Gospel has two parts.

The Person of Jesus and His Principles.

One is the life of God *within* you.

The other is the Law of God *around* you.

One is the *King*; and one is the *Kingdom*.

The *Person* of Jesus creates your *Peace*. His *Principles* create your *Prosperity*.

There is no relationship between God's love and your money. God loves many people who do not have money. Yet, many sincere lovers of God remain broke...

unable to pay their bills.

Who is deciding your Wealth?

God does not decide who has money. If God did, you would have to explain why the Mafia has money and missionaries do not.

The Person of Jesus Prepares You For Eternity; The Principles of Jesus Prepare You For The Earth. If you do not understand this truth, you will be puzzled... possibly embittered by the distribution of wealth on the earth.

The Laws of God even decide events on the earth. For instance, you will often hear people question, "I wonder why the hurricane went over there? I wonder why the storm hit that city?" The Bible clearly states that even winds obey God. (See Matthew 8:27.)

Ah, the plague of stupid! My greatest fear of hell is not the *fire*, but all the *fools* being in one place for all eternity. The pain of hell may not really be the fire. It will be the *fools* present! Think of how you react right now to one fool. Now, imagine all of them surrounding you...for *eternity!*

The Winds and the Sea obey Him. The crust at the bottom of the ocean creates the tsunami. The Bible says, "...the curse causeless shall not come," (Proverbs 26:2). There is always a cause. *Always.*

"Wisdom is the principal thing," (Proverbs 4:7). You may have thought faith or mercy was the principal thing. But, Solomon wrote, "Wisdom is the principal thing."

What is Wisdom? *Wisdom Is The Ability To Recognize Difference.* Joseph had the Wisdom to see Difference on the countenance of the butler and the baker. (See Genesis 40:1-14.) Joseph saw their distress and responded by asking, "What can I do for you?"

Every Problem Is An Invitation To A Relationship.

Wisdom is the ability to discern Difference...in a Moment. Remember the New Testament Miracle when the blind man cried out, "Jesus, Thou Son of David, have Mercy on me." (See Luke 18:37-38.) He discerned that the Presence of Jesus created a *difference* in that moment.

Wisdom is the ability to discern the Difference...in an Opportunity. The woman who had hemorrhaged for 12 years said, "If I can touch the hem of His garment I know I will be made whole." (See Matthew 9:20-22.) Jesus had no plans for her that day, but *she had a plan.*

There are many people who go through life saying, "I wonder what God wants?"

However, God is saying, "What do *you* want?"

Jesus looked at the blind man, "What would you have Me do?" The blind man had to declare his need.

Asking Is The Seed For Receiving.

Asking Is The Proof of Humility.

Asking Is The Only Evidence of Real Faith.

When Jesus hung between two thieves...only one discerned His Difference.

The prodigal son did not discern the Difference in the environment his father had created.

Never forget this: "Wisdom is the principal thing; therefore get Wisdom: and with all thy getting get understanding," (Proverbs 4:7).

There Are Two Ways To Get Wisdom: Mistakes And Mentors. The easiest way to get Wisdom is to *buy it.* A billionaire had an information pack priced at $1,000. There was a little black book in it that I could not buy anywhere else in the world. It contained so much knowledge.

I thought, "In two hours I can read that book and know what a man who is worth a billion dollars knows." For only $1,000, I found out in two hours what took him 70 years to discover.

Buy Wisdom.

Wisdom Keys To Remember

- ▶ *Every Problem Is Always A Wisdom Problem.*
- ▶ *Your Ignorance Is The Only Weapon Satan Possesses.*
- ▶ *Whatever You Are You Reproduce.*
- ▶ *Anything Unprotected Will Be Stolen.*
- ▶ *Every Loss Is The Seed For Restoration.*
- ▶ *Change Is Always Proportionate To Knowledge.*
- ▶ *Knowledge Is The Seed For Change.*
- ▶ *The Person of Jesus Prepares You For Eternity; The Principles of Jesus Prepare You For The Earth.*
- ▶ *Wisdom Is The Ability To Recognize Difference.*
- ▶ *Every Problem Is An Invitation To A Relationship.*
- ▶ *Asking Is The Seed For Receiving.*
- ▶ *Asking Is The Proof of Humility.*
- ▶ *Asking Is The Only Evidence of Real Faith.*
- ▶ *There Are Two Ways To Get Wisdom: Mistakes And Mentors.*

❧ 1 ❧

The Law of Difference

————————⟫▸●◂⟪————————

Your Difference Decides Your Importance.

The first Law that you must honor is The Law of Difference. What has God put inside of you that you do not see in others? That Difference is critical. *Something Within You Cannot Be Found In Another.*

Your Similarity Creates Your Comfort.

Your Difference Creates Your Rewards.

What do you love to *do?* What do you love to *think* about...*know* about...*learn* about? That is a clue to your Assignment on the earth.

I enjoy my moments with Dr. Morris Cerullo and his wife, Teresa. They are the same loving couple in the privacy of their home as they are in a public restaurant. After 57 years of marriage, he still reaches over and strokes her hand. She does not look like she resents it either! What a woman! He *saw* Difference.

If you do not know your distinctive Difference, you will never discern what others need from you. You become a hostage to trying to be what somebody wants you to be...instead of *who* you really are. Imagine the eternal task of teaching a cat to bark! A thousand years later, no progress has been made.

Study yourself. You must discover what your Difference is.

The Greatest Mind in the universe designed you.

You are the resulting product...of a billion years of thinking!

God placed a part of Himself in you that nobody else possesses. That is what has kept Him protecting you. Preserving you.

A million demons have sought to kill you. And totally failed, because of the Forever-God committed to accompanying you to the conclusion of your Assignment. Satan has sent assassin after assassin, strategy after strategy, but you are *still* alive and focused; full of The Spirit of God. Satan has failed in every single attempt to destroy you. His discourage-ment in his failures toward you is 1,000 times greater than you have ever felt.

Hell fears your Difference. And, stays aware of it.

Do not live the rest of your life without discerning the Investment God has placed in you. Something keeps God intrigued with you. Angels discuss you hourly.

You are the Carrier of His Presence. You are the carrier of His uniqueness.

Nobody understands you. Why are you confused by that? *How could they?* There has *never* been another you on the earth before!

What do you *love?*

What do you *hate?*

What *angers* you?

What makes you *weep?*

Is there a more important subject on the earth among humans than you? *Study you.*

The Law of Difference.

What does God like about you? Everything was created for His pleasure. You are making God feel good.

Wisdom Keys To Remember

▶ *Your Difference Decides Your Importance.*
▶ *Something Within You Cannot Be Found In Another.*
▶ *Your Similarity Creates Your Comfort.*
▶ *Your Difference Creates Your Rewards.*

RECOMMENDED INVESTMENTS:
The Law of Recognition (Book/B-114/248 pg)
The Uncommon Achiever (Book/B-133/128 pg)
The Wisdom Commentary, Vol. 1 (Book/B-136/256 pg)
The Law of Difference: How It Can Help You Succeed (CD/WCPL-14)

Your Self-Portrait
Determines
Your Self-Conduct.

-MIKE MURDOCK

☞ 2 ☜

THE LAW OF THE MIND

Every Life-Battle Is A Mind-Battle.

If you win in your Mind, you will win in life. If you lose in your Mind, you will lose in life. Whether you are a weightlifter in the Olympics or a karate expert...*it is all in the Mind.*

When you can manage your Mind, you can manage your life. Every battle is in the Mind. You win or lose in the Mind. "Let this mind be in you, which was also in Christ Jesus," (Philippians 2:5). This is why we must renew and purge the Mind.

3 Things Your Mind Needs

1.   *Your Mind Needs A Focus.*

You need to focus on something in your Future.

Your Mind has two parts: your Memory and your Imagination.

Your Memory Replays The Past; Your Imagination Preplays Your Future. God gives you pictures of Tomorrow so you will not regress and deteriorate into the Past. God says I will do a *new* thing. (See Isaiah 43:19.) Always remember your Mind must have a focus.

I love New. *New..!* Yes, shopping is energizing, exciting! I saw a book that said *Real Men Hate Shopping.* That was when I found out I must be part woman...because I really *like* shopping! *I like new.*

New *shirts*...new *ties*...new *cars*. I do not like anything refurbished, nor *almost* new.

God gave me a new *heart*...a new *life*. Old things have *passed* away. That means there has been a funeral for everything *used*. He said, "I will do a *new* thing."

God is a Creator.

You will need a picture...of your new Future.

That is why when God talks to you He will put a picture in your Mind of your Future. "Abraham, see the stars. That is what your children are going to be like... see the sand on the seashore. That is what your descendants are going to be like." (See Genesis 15:5; 22:17.)

The picture in your Mind controls your behavior. *You Will Always Act Like The Person You Think You Are.*

The first thing God will do when He wants to bless you is present a picture of how He sees you.

The shortest child in the smallest family in the runt tribe of Israel was hiding in the corner of a threshing floor and God said, "Gideon thou mighty man of valor."

Gideon moaned back, "Me?"

"Yes, you!" (See Judges 6:11-16.)

Jeremiah said, "I am a child."

God said, "Shut up. You are a prophet!" (See Jeremiah 1:8-12.)

You must act like the person God said you are.

Your picture of God will not bring great changes in some parts of your life. It is vital to picture yourself the way *He sees you.*

Scholars call this...your *Self-Portrait. Your Self-Portrait Determines Your Self-Conduct.*

2. *Your Mind Needs An Instruction.*

Speak to your Mind to harness your thinking. Your Mind does not filter the information it acquires. Your Mind is literally an Emotional Magnet searching for information to verify your opinion or to escape present pain.

Why do you keep reading the back of the same cereal box? Your Mind is *looking* for information...in desperation for *new*.

You will sit with people you do not enjoy for an hour just to hear something you need. *Something You Need May Be Hidden In Someone You Do Not Enjoy.*

Your Mind is on the prowl for Knowledge.

Your Mind requires an instruction. *"Tell me 7 reasons I will succeed this year. Tell me 7 reasons why my finances will double in 12 months."* Your Mind will gather that data.

3.   *Your Mind Needs A Hero.*

You need a Champion...that excites you.

You need an Example. Abraham was an example to Isaac and Jacob. Elijah unleashed passion in Elisha. Ruth loved the presence of Naomi. Two are better than one. That equation is Divine and unchanging.

At dinner, Peter J. Daniels, the famous billionaire from Australia explained the major secret to his uncommon success. "After my conversion to Christ, I read 7,000 biographies. I can quote almost every speech of Winston Churchill word for word."

Your Hero decides your energy, endurance and experiences. Find one. Anyone who has succeeded where you want to succeed; anyone who has conquered what you long to master.

Your Mind is your Garden. It is where you grow the fruit that sustains you. You are the gardener. You must kill the snakes and pull the weeds. You choose the flowers that sustain the fragrance. Guard your Garden...*relentlessly, ferociously and victoriously.*

Wisdom Keys To Remember

▶ *Every Life-Battle Is A Mind-Battle.*

▶ *Your Memory Replays The Past; Your Imagination Preplays Your Future.*

▶ *You Will Always Act Like The Person You Think You Are.*

▶ *Your Self-Portrait Determines Your Self-Conduct.*

▶ *Something You Need May Be Hidden In Someone You Do Not Enjoy.*

RECOMMENDED INVESTMENTS:
The Mentor's Manna On Attitude (Book/B-58/32 pg)
The Making of A Champion (Book/B-59/128 pg)
The 3 Most Important Things In Your Life (Book/B-101/240 pg)
The Wisdom Commentary, Vol. 2 (Book/B-220/312 pg)

❧ 3 ❧

THE LAW OF RECOGNITION

Anything You Fail To Recognize Will Exit Your Life.
This Law is so powerful, I felt stirred to write over 200 pages in my book: *The Law of Recognition.* Visit my website at WisdomOnline.com and you will find this in my collection. It is revolutionary.

Recognition of a Mentor. The Pharisees did not recognize that Jesus was the Christ, but Zacchaeus did. Elisha recognized Elijah's Difference.

Recognition of a passionate protégé. A protégé is very different from a parasite. A parasite wants you to *sponsor* them and pay their bills. A protégé wants you to *direct, teach* and *train* them. *Parasites Want What Is In Your Hand; Protégés Want What Is In Your Heart.*

Elisha was Elijah's uncommon protégé. (See 2 Kings 2.) Ruth was Naomi's uncommon protégé. (See Ruth 1:16.) They both *recognized* the Difference in their Mentors.

During the 1860's, a couple sold their farm so they could search for gold. They traveled around the world. Years later, they arrived in England...*bankrupt.*

Years had passed. They decided to go back to their farmhouse in America and see what it looked like. They found a barbed wire fence around their farm, with armed guards surrounding their property.

The second largest gold mine on the North American continent, Sutter's Mill had been discovered...

under their farmhouse.

Can you imagine their horror? They had sold their farm to search for gold, yet the entire time it had been right there under their home.

An interesting story came out in a major paper. A man noticed a $2.39 picture frame at a flea market. He loved the frame, but hated the picture. When he got home, he took out the picture to replace it. There was another picture behind the ugly one. He thought, "This looks different. This looks like the work of a professional."

When he called the museum, he was instructed to bring it in for evaluation. They did some research and discovered it was the work of a famous painter. He sold it for $11 million...*from a $2.39 picture frame.*

Something You Are Not Seeing Is Costing You.

Humility is not a personality trait.

Humility is not intimidation.

Humility Is Recognition of What You Do Not Have.

Humility causes you to search.

Those who never ask questions, research or read are often arrogant. *The Proof of Humility Is The Willingness To Ask Questions.*

Wisdom Keys To Remember

- ▶ *Anything You Fail To Recognize Will Exit Your Life.*
- ▶ *Parasites Want What Is In Your Hand; Protégés Want What Is In Your Heart.*
- ▶ *Something You Are Not Seeing Is Costing You.*
- ▶ *Humility Is Recognition of What You Do Not Have.*
- ▶ *The Proof of Humility Is The Willingness To Ask Questions.*

~ 4 ~

THE LAW OF TWO

Satan Never Showed Up Until Eve Did.

One cannot multiply. Adam could not multiply until Eve entered his life.

Demons do not multiply or have a bloodline. Demons are *not omnipresent.* Some days you do not feel demonic activity, and another day you may sense demonic opposition.

Demons are assigned *geographically.* Banks position their security guard where the treasure is.

Remember the amazing story of Daniel and the lions' den? He had another remarkable experience. He prayed for 21 days. At the end of 21 days, an angel appeared with the answer and said, "The day you prayed God dispatched me. I left His Presence and have been on the way to you for 21 days. I was hindered by an attempted interception. I had to call for Michael, one of the archangels from another province, to assist me."

The angel replied, "Then said he unto me, Fear not, Daniel: for from the first day that thou didst set thine heart to understand, and to chasten thyself before thy God, thy words were heard, and I am come for thy words. But the prince of the kingdom of Persia withstood me one and twenty days: but, lo, Michael, one of the chief princes, came to help me; and I remained there with the kings of Persia. Now I am come to make thee understand what shall befall thy people in the latter days: for yet the vision is for many days," (Daniel 10:12-14).

Get excited! When you feel demonic activity around your life, satan has just discovered the packages that have left the warehouses of Heaven. They have been released and are en route to you.

Your package is arriving soon.

Demonic activity is the clue that significant answers are about to explode in your life.

Be attentive to The Law of Two.

Jesus sent them out two by two. "Two are better than one...the threefold cord is not easily broken," (Ecclesiastes 4:9, 12).

When God gets ready for your Future, He will send an Intercessor...He will assign a Mentor...*an Elijah.*

Why is The Law of Two important?

I once read an amazing statistic. You are only 4 people away from any human on the earth. An example: One of the secret service men that ran every morning with former President Bush is one of the Partners to our ministry. He knows President Bush. President Bush knows someone else.

You are 4 people away from any human on the earth. God can get you anywhere He wants you in 24 hours. God does not use the calendar to access your Future.

He uses The Law of Two.

When God Wants To Bless You, He Brings A Person Into Your Life. Ruth was *one conversation* with Naomi away from her Boaz. David was *one enemy* away from the throne. You are only *one giant* away from taking care of the sheep manure of life and being in control of the host of the whole palace.

The Law of Two is about Agreement. "Again I say unto you, That if two of you shall agree on earth as touching any thing that they shall ask, it shall be done for them of My Father which is in Heaven," (Matthew 18:19).

Wisdom Key To Remember

▶ *When God Wants To Bless You, He Brings A Person Into Your Life.*

RECOMMENDED INVESTMENTS:
The Double Diamond Principle (Book/B-39/148 pg)
The Holy Spirit Handbook (Book/B-100/153 pg)
The Law of Recognition (Book/B-114/248 pg)

Go Where You Are
Celebrated
Instead of Where You
Are Tolerated.

-MIKE MURDOCK

➤ 5 ➤

THE LAW OF PLACE

Places Matter.

God made places before He made people.

When you receive a Divine instruction, you are often sent to a specific *Place.*

It happened in the life of Elijah. "Arise, get thee to Zarephath," (1 Kings 17:9).

It happened in the life of Jesus and the Disciples. "An he will shew you a large upper room furnished and prepared: there make ready for us," (Mark 14:15).

It happened when The Holy Spirit birthed the early Church. "And, being assembled together with them, commanded them that they should not depart from Jerusalem, but wait for the promise of the Father, which, saith He, ye have heard of Me," (Acts 1:4).

It was the secret in the healing of a Syrian General. "And Elisha sent a messenger unto him, saying, Go and wash in the Jordan seven times, and thy flesh shall come again to thee, and thou shalt be clean," (2 Kings 5:10).

It was in the command of Jesus to a blind man. "And said unto him, Go, wash in the pool of Siloam, (which is by interpretation, Sent.) He went his way therefore, and washed, and came seeing," (John 9:7).

Places matter more than anyone ever dreams.

Your Provision is at a Place. Money does not follow

you. Money is waiting for you at The Place of Obedience.

Jesus asked, "Children have you any meat?"

The disciples replied, "We toiled all night and have caught nothing."

He said, "Cast your nets on the other side." (See John 21:3-6.)

One of the first 3 questions I ask someone with a financial problem is: Are you performing your best at your present Place of Assignment?

Your Blessing is waiting for you at a Place.

God uses financial increase as an *incentive* for Obedience. Everywhere you find God discussing money, He talks about Obedience. Every time God talks about Obedience, He talks about a Place.

God instructed Abraham, "Leave your kinfolks." God had arranged his Future...away from his Comfort Zone. (See Genesis 12.)

The Law of Place.

Everything You Want Is...Somewhere.

A *Place.*

I could never do what Dr. Morris Cerullo, the famed evangelist, does. I am in awe of him every time I am in his presence. He is very attentive to Divine instruction. I remember the morning we met in the hotel lobby and he shared, "God told me to put on the big coat."

God was talking to him about his Assignment on the earth. I do not know of anyone who has trained as many preachers and teachers as Dr. Cerullo. God has sent him to many *Places.* He knows well the importance of The Law of Place.

Even Jesus recognized that He was not welcome

in certain places. He left Nazareth and went to Capernaum. Jesus prepared His disciples for this. *Go Where You Are Celebrated Instead of Where You Are Tolerated.*

You belong *somewhere.*

You do not belong everywhere.

Jesus did not say, "If they reject you, go to the Jerusalem Barnes and Nobles and buy Dale Carnegie's book, *How to Win Friends and Influence People*; or buy a John Maxwell book on how to be a leader."

"And into whatsoever city or town ye shall enter, enquire who in it is worthy; and there abide till ye go thence. And when ye come into an house, salute it. And if the house be worthy, let your peace come upon it: but if it be not worthy, let your peace return to you. And whosoever shall not receive you, nor hear your words, when ye depart out of that house or city, shake off the dust of your feet," (Matthew 10:11-14).

The Law of Place.

You will succeed *somewhere.*

You will not succeed everywhere.

Have you found your Place? Somewhere…a Territory has your name on it. *Somewhere.* Every Territory is a reward from the Seed of Battle. *Battle Is The Seed For Territorial Order And Possession.*

Battles Are Appointments

The Timing of Warfare…Reveals The Importance of An Approaching Event. If unusual warfare surrounds your life, God has decided to assign Territory on the earth to you.

Giants Are Not Signs of Your Exit From Egypt; Giants Are Proofs of Your Entry Into Canaan.

The Israelites did not face the giants when they left Egypt. The battle was over the grapes of Canaan. When you see giants in your life, declare, "My Territory is here. God has brought me to such a Place."

The Law of Place.

Elijah did not use a *prayer cloth* for the missing raven. He did not *anoint* the dried up brook. He did not speak to the water, "Water come forth!" He did not view his trouble as something to endure, change or fight.

The season of that Place was over. "Arise, get thee to Zarephath," (1 Kings 17:9).

The Law of Place.

Never stay where God has not assigned you.

...your *weakness* will *flourish.*

...your *strength* will *die.*

...you will never be honored for your Difference... *when you are in the wrong place.*

What My Fish Taught Me

Some fish for my ponds were brought to my property. Before I placed them in the water, I stared at the fish as they lay on the grass. I thought, "Wow, they cannot talk...they cannot walk...they cannot fly. Fish must be stupid. Maybe we should stop eating fish!"

Then I picked up each fish and dropped them one by one in the water. Their movements were electrifying as they entered the environment perfect for the hidden Greatness within them.

Their genius was immediately apparent.

The Holy Spirit spoke to me, "When you are where I have assigned you, you have no competitors...*no rivals.* You are The Genius when you are in The Place...

where God has assigned you."

Your Assignment Is Always The Problem God Has Assigned You To Solve For Others.

Your Assignment is not everywhere...*it is to somewhere.*

Wisdom Keys To Remember

▶ *Everything You Want Is...Somewhere.*

▶ *Go Where You Are Celebrated Instead of Where You Are Tolerated.*

▶ *Battle Is The Seed For Territorial Order And Possession.*

▶ *The Timing of Warfare...Reveals The Importance of An Approaching Event.*

▶ *Giants Are Not Signs of Your Exit From Egypt; Giants Are Proofs of Your Entry Into Canaan.*

▶ *Your Assignment Is Always The Problem God Has Assigned You To Solve For Others.*

Recommended Investments:
The Assignment (The Dream & The Destiny) Vol. 1
    (Book/B-74/164 pg)
The Law of Recognition (Book/B-114/248 pg)
The Wisdom Commentary, Vol. 1 (Book/B-136/256 pg)

Honor Is The Willingness
To Magnify Difference
Instead of Weakness.

-MIKE MURDOCK

～ 6 ～

THE LAW OF HONOR

Every Sin On Earth Is A Sin of Dishonor.

Consider the Ten Commandments. The first 4 deal with honoring *God;* the last 6 deal with honoring *people.*

Honor is different from Wisdom.

Wisdom is the *recognition* of Difference. Right and wrong...righteousness and evil...God and satan.

Honor Is The Willingness To Reward Someone For Their Difference.

The Law of Honor is the most important Law on earth. Honor is not an Anointing, a Miracle nor an answer to prayer. It is your personal choice...to celebrate the distinctive Difference in another.

Honor Is A Qualifying Seed

Honor Is The Seed For Access Into Any Environment On Earth. Honor decides who desires you, accepts you and rewards you. *Honor Grows In Every Environment... In Every Single Season of Your Life.*

Honor Is The Willingness To Magnify Difference Instead of Weakness.

Flaws are Divine design, not a human choice. Your weaknesses are undeniable. They often disguise your Greatness. Every bloodline and family has a *history* of dysfunction. Is your *background* stained? Do you feel robbed of Excellence, Education or Example? Your decision to embrace The Law of Honor can compensate for whatever you lack genetically...and in intelligence.

Study The Law of Honor...around you.

Sow Honor as a Seed of Respect, Recognition.

Honor will compensate and silence all the doubts about every other weakness in your life. Honor will take you further than genius and all your experiences in life.

Jesus judged others by their willingness to show Honor. Mary demonstrated Honor when she washed the feet of Jesus. (See Matthew 26:7-13.)

Honor Has A Distinctive Fragrance

The Fragrance of Honor Is As Distinctive As The Odor of Dishonor. You cannot disguise the *stink* of a skunk; you cannot hide the *fragrance* of Honor. Countenance and conversation verifies Honor. You can talk to somebody 5 minutes and know their understanding of Honor.

Honor has a Sound...a *distinctive* Sound.

So, does Dishonor.

Listen for the sound of Honor. In family conversations, TV talk-show hosts and news reporters. Even resumés can be deceptive. You may have spent your entire life building relationships based on the *resumés* of people. Passion can be misleading. Do you know of anyone with a *greater* resumé than Lucifer? He worked next to God for *years!*

Never evaluate people by their *experience.*

Never evaluate people by their *passion.*

The Code of Honor

Evaluate people by their Code of Honor. Who have they chosen to honor...through their words, time or friendship? Who have they chosen to dishonor, ignore or trivialize? Whose voice have they chosen to trust? What is the character of those they admire?

Diligence in the workplace is proof of Honor.

Diligence Is Immediate Attention To An Instruction; Delayed Obedience Is The Proof of Dishonor.

When people show you what they are really like, believe them.

Honor is the bridge to any season you would like to enter. *Honor Is The Seed For Access.*

Oh, my Precious Friend, always *choose the path of Honor.* Always. I have some sad memories because I neglected to follow The Law of Honor.

If you *succeed* with your life, you will be able to trace it to those you chose to Honor. If you *fail* with your life, it can be traced to a person you chose to dishonor.

Rewarding Those Who Honor You

Those who Honor you qualify for a different relationship with you. A *closer* relationship. A *gracious* relationship. A *growing* relationship. A *long-term* relationship.

You may be a parent with 4 children. If I ask you, "Who has chosen to Honor you the most?" You will immediately imagine their countenance. Debate is unnecessary.

Note that I did not ask you, "Who do you love the most?" I did not ask you, "Who has been most affectionate?"

The question is worth asking every day of your life. "Who has shown me Honor?"

You will protect yourself if you are honest in asking this question also, "Who has shown me great dishonor?"

Personality is persuasive...and incredibly deceptive. But, the willingness to respect The Law of Honor will prevent a thousand nights, weeping from a broken heart.

Celebrate the Difference of those who carry the aroma of Honor. Never reward people according to their *need*. Respond to people proportionate to their *Honor*.

Jesus did not habitually go home with Pharisees to present them a seminar. He went home with Zacchaeus because of The Law of Honor. (See Luke 19:1-9.)

The Billionaire And His Housekeeper

A newspaper article fascinated me. Some months ago, a billionaire left $5 billion to his housekeeper. If I recall, he may have left $100 to each of his children to prevent them from contesting his will.

He left the entire inheritance to his housekeeper.

Ah, yes! Honor has a *sound*...an *aroma*...a *fragrance*...an *aura*. It dissolves discomfort, friction and unworthiness. It cures a lifetime of abuse...in a single moment.

Your friendship is an investment in another. It creates loss or gain. True friendship can become costly, in time, energy and even money. So, re-evaluate every relationship in your life by The Law of Honor. Do not study potential. Even Lucifer *had* potential!

Lucifer...The Son of Honor

Three angels received Divine Authority, Territorial Power and Leadership...Michael, Gabriel and Lucifer. (Leaders, when you distribute tasks, you must also delegate Authority.)

The original name for Lucifer meant son of Honor. Lucifer's Assignment was to *collect* all the Honor from the angels and *present* it to God.

Lucifer observed God receiving great Honor and *suddenly* pride entered him. It continues to be a mystery to me how he could become a devil *without* a devil to influence him. One day, he suddenly says, "I want that Honor for me." God reacted...with lightning speed. The battle was not lengthy, nor even disputable.

The Bible says God flung him like lightning to the earth. "And He said unto them, I beheld satan as lightning fall from Heaven," (Luke 10:18). "And there was war in Heaven: Michael and his angels fought against the dragon; and the dragon fought and his angels, And prevailed not; neither was their place found any more in Heaven. And the great dragon was cast out, that old serpent, called the devil, and satan, which deceiveth the whole world: he was cast out into the earth, and his angels were cast out with him," (Revelation 12:7-9).

Something within me wants to approach God with a question. "Why did you not give him a second chance? What stops you from offering mercy to someone who worked for you so long? You created words. You are a Master Conversationalist. The Best. You are a Persuader. You could have pulled Lucifer to the side and said, 'Hey buddy. You are off track. Come on now. This is Daddy's territory. I am The One who put you there. You need a little extra mentorship. Maybe we need more private time together.'"

God refused another minute of mentorship.

God saw him as a fool, unworthy of exchange.

God did not even think he was worthy of a conversation. Why?

Dishonor *disqualifies.*

Dishonor is *contagious.*

Dishonor *destroys.*

Dishonor *exposes* a Deceiver.
Lucifer *knew* too much.
Lucifer *saw* too much.
Lucifer *received* too much.

How To Recognize A Person of Dishonor

Deception Is The Birthplace For All Pain.
Remember the story of the prodigal son? The son sneered at the lifetime teaching and provision of his father. He even had the *inappropriate* boldness to ask for something he had not earned.

The First Clue To Dishonor Is The Request For Something Unearned. The father did not chase the prodigal son down the road begging him to return.

What You Refuse To Learn From People, You Must Learn Through Pain.
Dishonor is a choice...*a character decision.*

Restoration rarely occurs after a decision of dishonor has been made. Remember Judas? "Then Judas, which had betrayed Him, when he saw that He was condemned, repented himself, and brought again the thirty pieces of silver to the chief priests and elders, Saying, I have sinned in that I have betrayed the innocent blood. And they said, What is that to us? see thou to that. And he cast down the pieces of silver in the temple, and departed, and went and hanged himself," (Matthew 27:3-5).

Dishonor is not a character glitch that you are born with. Dishonor is a *decision* to defy and disrespect God.

The dominant reward of Wisdom is the ability to recognize who should be honored. The first commandment with a promise of a reward is the fifth commandment to honor your parents. Ask God to show you who to honor...and to identify anyone who willingly dishonors you.

Honor can be taught.

I urge you to do a 90-day campaign killing snakes and pulling weeds to make your Garden what it ought to be. Do not leave any snake alive in your Garden.

Let wrong relationships die. Wrong people never leave *voluntarily*. Like Jonah, you have to shove them overboard...toward the big fish! Read the story again. (See Jonah 1:5-17).

The Law of Honor.

Marriages fail because of the lack of Honor.

Marriages do not fail because of unfaithfulness. Unfaithfulness occurred because there was no *heart of honor.*

Honor is a *Decision.*

Honor is a *Seed.*

Honor is a *Law.*

Identify disrespect. Change any part of your life where there has been dishonor.

Teach honor to the trainable. If someone simply does not know The Law of Honor, you can train them.

Never ignore the decision of a rebel. If someone has relentlessly rebelled against your *example,* your *investment* and your *warnings* release them to God.

Observe the Divine reaction of God to Ephraim. "Ephraim is joined to idols: let him alone," (Hosea 4:17).

God permits people the right to choose. "As it is written, Jacob have I loved, but Esau have I hated," (Romans 9:13).

Wisdom Keys To Remember

▶ *Every Sin On Earth Is A Sin of Dishonor.*
▶ *Honor Is The Willingness To Reward Someone For Their Difference.*

▶ *Honor Is The Seed For Access Into Any Environment In Every Season.*

▶ *Honor Grows In Every Environment...In Every Single Season of Your Life.*

▶ *Honor Is The Willingness To Magnify Difference Instead of Weakness.*

▶ *The Fragrance of Honor Is As Distinctive As The Odor of Dishonor.*

▶ *Diligence Is Immediate Attention To An Instruction; Delayed Obedience Is The Proof of Dishonor.*

▶ *Honor Is The Seed For Access.*

▶ *Deception Is The Birthplace For All Pain.*

▶ *The First Clue To Dishonor Is The Willingness To Ask For Something You Are Unwilling To Earn.*

❧ 7 ❧

THE LAW OF THE SEED

A Seed...Is A Beginning.
The Bible is a book about The Law of The Seed.
Words Are The Seeds...For Feelings.
Mercy Is The Seed...For Change.
Honor Is The Seed...For Access.
Gratitude Is The Seed...For More.
Whatever you are thankful for *will* increase.

Jesus was a Seed. Think about this for a moment. God had a Son, but, He wanted a Family. So, He planted His Son...on Calvary, to create His Family... His Eternal Harvest.

Prophets understood The Law of The Seed. Elijah looked at the widow of Zarephath and said, "Bring me a little meal."

She said, "I have just enough for me and my son."

Elijah did not say, "Wrong house. I am so sorry."

Instead, he looked at her and began to paint the picture of her Harvest on her Mind. "What you bring to me will be the Seed. Throughout this famine, you will not lack." (See 1 Kings 17:10-16.)

Was Jesus Serious About This?

Jesus taught His disciples The Law of The Seed. Remember His conversation with Peter? Peter complained to Jesus, "We have given up everything to follow You."

Jesus could have reacted, "Right! Three catfish and a boat." But, He did not. Jesus looked at him and said, "Anything you give up for Me will be returned to you one hundred-fold." (See Mark 10:28-30.) *One hundred-fold.*

A minister friend said, "Mike, I do not think Jesus really *meant* one hundred-fold."

I humorously responded, "When you get to Heaven, you may host a Conversation Seminar for Jesus to teach Him how to talk. Do you think He just got carried away *in the moment*, afraid Peter was going to quit the ministry, so He yelled *one hundred-fold?*"

Important Reminders

The Law of The Seed Simply Means Something You Have Been Given Will Create Anything Else You Have Been Promised.

There will never be a day in your life that you have nothing.

Inventory your Seeds instead of your *needs.*

Never study what is *missing* in your life.

Study what you already *possess.*

Something You Have Been Given Will Create Anything Else You Have Been Promised.

Wrap *expectation* around your Seed.

Give your Seed an *Assignment.*

A man told me years ago, "Dr. Murdock, when I give I expect *nothing* in return."

I replied, "I wrote a little song for you. *How dumb thou art! How dumb thou art!*"

My Conversation With Oral Roberts

I will never forget a conversation I had years ago

with Oral Roberts, as we drove around Tulsa, Oklahoma. I was in my thirties at the time. "Dr. Roberts, what is the single greatest secret you have ever learned in your whole ministry?"

"Mike, I do not think anybody has ever asked me that." Then he said, "Sowing my Seed for a desired result. Learn to give your Seed an Assignment."

The Ex-Husband And The Seed

It happened in Houston, Texas.

I was tired. The service was over. A woman walked up to me after I had received an Offering. I had just told the people *to write on their checks* wherever they needed to see a Harvest...the most in their personal life.

She said, "My ex-husband has not paid me child support in 15 years."

My first thought was, "I do not think he is going to start now." But, when I looked at her face she seemed so happy and expectant. I thought, "I cannot go back on the word from The Lord about Expectation."

I said, rather boldly, "Did you put his name on the check?"

She replied confidently, "Yes, I did."

Her Miracle started 14 days later. She received her first check from him for $65,000. She had given her Seed an Assignment.

The $58 Husband!

It happened on a Sunday night.

I was in Daytona Beach, Florida, receiving a Seed-Faith Offering for the work of the Lord. The Holy Spirit impressed me to share my personal testimony about sowing a Seed for $58 in Washington, D.C. (The 58 represented how many different kinds of blessing I had counted in The Bible.)

"Write on your check exactly where you want to see a Harvest," I instructed everybody. *"Talk* to your Seed. *Speak* to your Seed where you want to see a Harvest. *Target* your Seed. *Give* your Seed an Assignment."

There was a young man on the platform who wrote on his check...*a gorgeous wife.* There was a young lady on the back seat of the church who wrote on her check...*a godly husband.* They had not met each other before.

They met a few days later. Eventually, they got married and had several children.

One day I was at their house for a meal. She said rather wryly, "Dr. Murdock, tell people to be real careful what they write on those checks!"

One Moment Can Decide A Lifetime

One meal with Jesus changed Zacchaeus forever.
One conversation with Elijah changed the widow.
One Seed of Faith can unleash a forever Harvest.

There have been 8 levels of Seed-sowing that I have seen radical Harvest; instant, quick, swift, within weeks. The quickest and greatest Harvest out of every Seed I have ever sowed has been on a $1,000 Seed for whatever reason.

I shared this on television in a passionate Moment, while The Spirit of God stirred me. An anointing came upon me in the middle of a television program. I said, "There is somebody watching me. You are facing a lawsuit. *Sow a Seed of $1,000.* Write on your check where you would like to see a Harvest."

There was a couple watching me in Wilmington, Delaware, right across from Philadelphia. They were being sued for $80,000. Less than 30 days after they sowed their Seed, the $80,000 lawsuit was cancelled. They received a check for $40,000.

A Profound Miracle In New York

I was meeting privately with about 300 of my strongest partners in New York City. A couple seated to my left started crying. They were local pastors. The wife stood up and said, "Can I share something?"

I said, "Sure."

"We have been watching you for years on TV. Some months ago, you told us how you broke the back of poverty with a $1,000 Seed. Something leaped in our hearts and we decided we would borrow $1,000 from someone to sow. Within 30 days we received over $100 million for our ministry. We were able to pay the $4 million we owed on our church."

Their testimony is profound.

The key is *focusing* your Seed.

Someone asked me, "Did you feel happy over their $100 million?" Well, I had mixed feelings. I was puzzled why God has never done that for me!

Your Next Season Is One Seed Away!

My debt-free house was birthed from a Seed.

At a conference in Chicago, Illinois, a preacher stood and said, "How many would like to be debt-free?"

I laughed inwardly. I thought to myself, *"There are a lot of people who are debt-free. The homeless are already debt-free. I can get you debt-free in 30 minutes. You can give up your house and car...and you can be debt-free fast."*

The preacher then continued, "How many would like a debt-free house? Plant a Seed equal to one month's mortgage payment. Write on the left hand corner of the check...*debt-free house in 12 months.* Hold your check in your left hand. Slap it 3 times."

I smiled inwardly with a humorous thought, "That sounds a little witchcrafty to me!"

But, I knew that he was a man of God. No doubt about that. *My Reaction To A Man of God Determines God's Reaction To Me.*

God-Instructions are not necessarily logical. He gives you a Mind to do logical stuff for yourself.

If You Can Understand A God-Instruction, It Was Not A God-Instruction.

When God talks to you about the walls falling down, He may say walk around them 7 days in a row and 7 times on Sunday. (See Joshua 6.)

Sometimes, God gives *crazy* instructions to verify your faith in Him and His nature.

In 8 months, my house was supernaturally debt-free.

The Law of the Seed means something I *have* is the Golden Key to anything I *want*.

Something I Have Been Given Will Unlock Anything I Have Been Promised.

Newspapers have criticized me because of the manifestation of The Blessing on my life. They have taken pictures of my jet and my home. They have sneered, "He says when you sow a Seed you can expect a Harvest." Yet, they print pictures of the Harvest for free in their newspaper. *Isn't that a little weird?*

During a meal with Dr. Oral Roberts, The Holy Spirit said to me, "Give him $25,000."

I thought, "I must have intercepted a memo. Surely, God is telling him to give me $25,000."

At the time, I did not remember the words of Ezekiel...*sow up so the blessing can come down.*

"And the first of all the firstfruits of all things, and every oblation of all, of every sort of your oblations, shall be the priest's: ye shall also give unto the priest the first of your dough, *that he may cause the blessing* to rest in thine house," (Ezekiel 44:30).

You Must Sow Up For The Blessing To Come Down.
Every Blessing Has A Cause.
Every Seed Has A Different Future.

Finally, at the end of the meal I said, "Dr. Roberts, I am going to drive to my office and get a check." It took me an hour and a-half to get back to the hotel where he was staying.

As he held the check in his hand, he asked, "What is the biggest need you have in your life? We are going to *focus* this Seed toward that need."

That happened on a Sunday afternoon.

By Tuesday, there was an explosion of Miracles.

You Are One Seed Away From Something You Have Been Passionately Pursuing.

A few days after I had planted my first $1,000 Seed, a man gave me $10,000. I was preaching in New Orleans.

God said, "I want you to plant that $10,000."

I explained to God that it was my Harvest because I had just received it. However, I obeyed and sowed it that night. Five days later, I received a call from two of the greatest Christian Television networks in America. They gave me free air-time for years...which *launched* my Partnership and Ministry.

I was with the famous life coach and teacher, Paula White. She said, "Mike, you do know how this ministry got started?"

I said, "No."

She said, "I had nothing. Nobody would give me one penny for my ministry. I went to hear you teach and that night you said, 'There is somebody here God is instructing to give everything you have.'" She planted everything she had that night as a Seed into the work of God.

Within 24 hours, a lady gave her $15,000.

She launched her worldwide ministry.

You Are One Seed Away From Everything You Want.

What has God told you to sow?

What Seed remains unplanted?

What secret fear has aborted your Harvest?

Something In Your Hand Controls Your Future.

My Prayer For 3 Harvests To Enter Your Life

1. Twenty-Four Months of Financial Authority.

Financial Authority differs from Financial Breakthrough.

A Breakthrough is an *experience.*

A Miracle has an *ending.*

An Anointing is *movement* for a reason.

Authority is a *position* of control and influence.

Let's agree together:

For the next 24 months, you will be the Financial Authority in every environment that you enter. Everything has to bow to the anointing that is on the inside of you.

You will experience 24 months of unprecedented Financial Authority.

God will give you *Financial Ideas.*

God will give you *Financial Breakthroughs.*

God will give you *Financial Anointing.*

God will give you *Financial Authority.*

You will be a walking magnet for Financial Favor.

You are one person away from your Future.

It is not about how *many* people like you.

It is about *who* likes you.

Joseph did not need all of Egypt voting for him. He just needed Pharaoh to say, "I like you."

"And the thing was good in the eyes of Pharaoh, and in the eyes of all his servants. And Pharaoh said unto his servants, Can we find such a one as this is, a man in whom the Spirit of God is? And Pharaoh said unto Joseph, Forasmuch as God hath shewed thee all this, there is none so discreet and wise as thou art: Thou shalt be over my house, and according unto thy word shall all my people be ruled: only in the throne will I be greater than thou. And Pharaoh said unto Joseph, See, I have set thee over all the land of Egypt. And Pharaoh took off his ring from his hand, and put it upon Joseph's hand, and arrayed him in vestures of fine linen, and put a gold chain about his neck; And he made him to ride in the second chariot which he had; and they cried before him, Bow the knee: and he made him ruler over all the land of Egypt. And Pharaoh said unto Joseph, I am

Pharaoh, and without thee shall no man lift up his hand or foot in all the land of Egypt. And Pharaoh called Joseph's name Zaphnath-paaneah; and he gave him to wife Asenath the daughter of Potipherah priest of On. And Joseph went out over all the land of Egypt," (Genesis 41:37-45).

Esther did not need everybody to like her. The only person whose opinion mattered was the king...and he liked her. "And the king loved Esther above all the women, and she obtained grace and favour in his sight more than all the virgins; so that he set the royal crown upon her head, and made her queen instead of Vashti," (Esther 2:17).

Say this aloud: "I am a receiver of Financial Authority. I will master The Law of the Harvest. I will master The Law of Receiving."

2. Seven-Fold Return of Anything Satan Has Stolen. God will restore things you did not know you had lost. It may be through an insurance settlement, a legacy, an investment that appeared to have failed or through the government.

Expect a seven-fold return.

"But if he be found, he shall restore sevenfold; he shall give all the substance of his house," (Proverbs 6:31).

Come into Agreement with me. I set myself with Agreement for a seven-fold return of everything satan has stolen from you...joy, health, relationships or Favor. I pray a seven-fold return, not just on your finances, but on everything satan has stolen from you...even your *credibility* and *reputation.*

Expect Restoration of everything he has withheld from your life.

3. Favor With A Financial Boaz.

Favor is currency...in any environment on earth.

Favor opens doors you thought would never open. Favor accelerates you to the center of wherever you want to be. Favor brings celebration of your Difference.

One Day of Favor Is Worth A Thousand Days of Labor. You cannot work hard enough to get everything you want. You will need Favor in your life.

Joseph Only Needed Favor From Just One Person. "Thou shalt be over my house, and according unto thy word shall all my people be ruled: only in the throne will I be greater than thou. And Pharaoh said unto Joseph, See, I have set thee over all the land of Egypt," (Genesis 41:40-41).

Ruth Only Needed Favor From One Man To Change Her World. "Then she said, Let me find favour in thy sight, my lord; for that thou hast comforted me, and for that thou hast spoken friendly unto thine handmaid, though I be not like unto one of thine handmaidens. And Boaz said unto her, At mealtime come thou hither, and eat of the bread, and dip thy morsel in the vinegar. And she sat beside the reapers: and he reached her parched corn, and she did eat, and was sufficed, and left. And when she was risen up to glean, Boaz commanded his young men, saying, Let her glean even among the sheaves, and reproach her not: And let fall also some of the handfuls of purpose for her, and leave them, that she may glean them, and rebuke her not. So she gleaned in the field until even, and beat out that she had gleaned: and it was about an ephah of barley," (Ruth 2:13-17).

Seize Favor like a coat. Wrap it around yourself. Do not let it go. Decide to be the *carrier* of Divine Favor.

Decide…to *attract* Favor.
Decide…to *sow* Favor.
Decide…to *reap* Favor.
Declare that you are a walking *magnet* for Favor.
Say these words: "I *attract* Favor. I *declare* Favor. I *speak* Favor. I *walk* in Favor."

Explanation of The Boaz Anointing

It happened in the Anatole Hotel in Dallas, Texas.

I was praying for those who had come forward to plant a Seed-Faith Offering into the work of The Lord. As I stood in front of a lady, God said, "Tell her I am going to give her a *Boaz Anointing.*"

I had never heard of such a thing. So, while everybody was praying, I asked the Lord, "What do You mean by a *Boaz Anointing?*"

He began to describe Ruth. She so valued the Anointing…the Difference in Boaz…that everything he owned and possessed actually came into her life. She eventually gave birth to Obed, who fathered Jesse, who fathered David, who fathered Solomon, who ushered in the lineage of Jesus.

The Holy Spirit inspired me to pray, "Because you have honored and respected the Anointing on this ministry for Divine Wisdom and Financial Prosperity, I agree that you will receive the same blessing on your own life. According to your faith may God give you the same Miracles and experiences every time He gives them to me. In Jesus' Name, I decree it so."

Well, that is a little bold. It certainly took a special touch from The Lord to enter into that special kind of covenant with people I did not even know. I simply knew that their Seed was a conversation in the

Heavens, and was proof of their uncommon Faith in their Partnership with God.

That is where it began. I began to pray for others to receive the Boaz Anointing...*every time God blessed me, He would bless them.* Every time God gave me a jet, He would bless them with a jet. Every time God gave me a car, He would bless them with a car.

Something happens at different levels of faith that is unexplainable, but quite glorious. Significant and unforgettable Harvests have exploded in my life at 8 different levels of Seed-sowing.

My swiftest Harvests have always come from Seeds of $1,000. If God ever makes it possible for you to sow a Seed of $1,000, be swift to obey Him. Avoid negotiation, and delays. Only a fool will negotiate with a giver. (By the way, there are many wonderful ministries worthy of that Seed.)

I do not know where that Seed of $1,000 may be stored in your home, savings or in a future account. You may have money set aside for a trip to Israel or for a vacation. You may have set aside finances for another car or equity in your home.

One thing I know, the Anointing on the Seed of $1,000 is explosive and unlike any other Seed you have ever planted. *You will never regret it. Ever.*

Your Seed Can Go Where You Cannot Go.

Your Seed will drive back the spiritual darkness that has surrounded your life. You may not be called to jump on planes, sleep in small hotel rooms and travel to the 4 corners of the earth. But, you can be one of those who holds up the ladder...and helps pull in the net for those who are the deliverers of those in captivity.

Sit down now...and make a decision to focus your

Seed of $1,000...in Divine Partnership with God. Everything you have came from Him anyway. He has given you Seed to sow...not hoard. *What You Keep Is Your Harvest; What You Sow Is Your Seed.*

Make it a *Soul-Winning* Seed.

Make it a *Mission* Seed.

Make it an *Evangelism* Seed.

Make it a *Partnership* Seed.

Make it a *Jesus* Seed.

This Seed of $1,000 will cause millions to hear the Name of Jesus. For the rest of your life, you can know your Seed of $1,000 brought The Gospel to the nations of the earth.

Sending The Gospel around the world is not my only focus. I want to see these 3 Harvests rush toward you. I have felt stirred over the last few weeks for 24 months of unprecedented financial breakthrough for the family of God.

You are entering an Investor's Paradise.

You are entering the World of Favor.

America will experience judgment like the Egyptians when the Israelites left.

But not at your house.

You see, God uses problems among the Egyptians in the palace to summon the Josephs from the prison.

Joseph Did Not Have A Future Until The King Had A Problem. The current Global Crisis is a glorious incubator for the promotion of God's family.

My Prayer Over Your Seed of $1,000...And The Boaz Anointing

Please pray this prayer aloud with me...

"Holy Spirit, I ask You for the greatest 24 months

of Harvest we have ever had. We will have Favor. We will have a seven-fold return on everything satan has stolen. We will have debt-free homes. We will have household salvation. Children we thought would never come to You are going to be set free from drugs and alcohol. We are going to see Your glory. I ask You for a Boaz Anointing.

"Let my Precious Friend know that $1,000 is not enough to keep. One thousand dollars will not buy a house. One thousand dollars will not buy a car. There is very little we can do with $1,000. But, when we put it in Your hand, You will breathe on that Seed.

"*We give this Seed an Assignment.* We call in not only the salvation of people in Nigeria and Brazil, but we call in the salvation of every member of our family. *What we make happen for others, You will make happen for us. What we make happen for a man of God, You will make happen for us.*

"Father, I ask You to do something ridiculously wonderful within 8 days for my Precious Partner who will be sowing this Seed. I decree it in Jesus' Name."

Wave a hand to God and say, "God, do something so ridiculous and glorious as the first wave of my Harvest. Let this Seed of $1,000 be my Turning-Point Seed."

The Lifetime Blessing Seed

Dr. Myles Monroe called sometime ago and reminded me of a couple in his church. I had given my testimony at the Diplomat Center in Bahamas of how God had given me a lifetime income from a one-time Seed of $8,500. They had walked up to me and said, "We want God to give us a lifetime income."

It happened 21 days later. They made a profit of

$17 million...*in one transaction on the Internet.*

I was in Costa Rica some weeks ago and while I was giving my testimony, a man and his wife walked up to the front. A pastor behind me said, "Let them come forward. They are legitimate."

The man started giving his testimony.

"Two years ago, my business was bankrupt. I was going out of business. Mike Murdock came to Costa Rica and he anointed me for God to bless me."

(I have asked the Lord to raise up 300 millionaires under our ministry. We have 20 so far.)

He continued, "I wanted to be a millionaire. I was broke and going bankrupt. From the time Mike Murdock anointed me with oil, God has given me 5 businesses. I just sold the first one for $160 million. I am selling the other 4 because I have decided to be a preacher. I do not need anymore money. I am starting a church out of $160 million from my first business."

God said He will "...give seed to the sower, and bread to the eater," (Isaiah 55:10). "Now He that ministereth seed to the sower both minister bread for your food, and multiply your seed sown, and increase the fruits of your righteousness," (2 Corinthians 9:10).

I do not consider a million dollars to be a whole lot of money. Once God starts dreaming through you a million is just for getting started.

I have never heard of another ministry praying for anybody to receive a Lifetime Blessing Seed. This is something God did for me on a Sunday night in Columbus, Ohio. All I had to my name was $8,500.

God said, "Would you like to explore and experiment with what I could do with your $8,500?"

Six weeks later at 7:15 on a Tuesday morning, at the Hyatt Regency Hotel in Houston, Texas, God gave me an idea. It went around the world. God blessed me beyond my wildest dreams and imagination through a one-time Seed of $8,500.

Someone asked one time, "What made you plant a Seed that large?"

I said, *"That Seed was not as big as my dream.* My dream is a lot bigger than $8,500."

If God is talking to you about the $8,500 Seed, let me encourage you never to negotiate with a Giver. God will give you more than you ever dreamed. I have paid cash for a Rolls Royce because of that $8,500 Seed. I was able to build a gymnasium at my house from that $8,500 Seed. I look back and remember how I actually fought *mentally* over keeping that Seed, but God was giving me an *Opportunity.*

The best thing you can give somebody is an Opportunity to wrap their faith around a Seed.

My Prayer Over Your Lifetime Blessing Seed of $8,500

"Lord, I do not know their background. I do not know what they are facing, but I sanctify this Mission Seed of $8,500 as the beginning of the most glorious days of their life. I ask for wave after wave of blessing before this year ends.

"Let my Precious Partner see investments prosper and restore back in their lives money they thought they had lost.

"I speak to this Seed of $8,500 for the sake of The Gospel as the beginning of the greatest season of their whole life. It is not that they do not need the $8,500, they need the Harvest from it far more. It may be money set aside for retirement or for buying a vacation home or rental property.

"Use this Seed to *silence* every Absalom in their business; every Judas in their relationships. Use this Seed to *mute* the voice of every adversary. This is going to be the Seed that *destroys* the voice of the Goliath in their life. I sanctify it in Jesus' Name. Amen."

My Closing Thought To You

My life is a collection of Miracles.

The Holy Spirit changed me forever in a dramatic encounter on July 13, 1994...at 7 a.m. *His Voice is the most important Voice in your life.* He is The Source of your Wisdom...and every good thing that you desire. Establish a *place* and *time* where you meet with Him each morning. Stay *attentive* to His whispers since He never screams. Walk in total *obedience* with your Tithe and Offerings planted as Seeds with *expectation* of a Harvest. Avoid strife at all costs. Stay *thankful*. Lavish the Seeds of Honor and Integrity into your immediate environment. Embrace every Law of God with Expectation of a Reward. Expect your Financial Partnership to bring eventual and unstoppable blessing, in Jesus' Name.

I look forward to hearing from you and what this book has meant to your life. When you write me, ask for your Gift Copy of my magazine, *The Wisdom Digest*. You can watch my Daily Wisdom-Talk on my website at...WisdomOnline.com. I would love to meet you face-to-face here at our conferences at The Wisdom Center.

Always Pursuing The Wisdom of God,

Mike Murdock

Wisdom Keys of Mike Murdock In This Book

1. A Seed...Is A Beginning.
2. Anything Unprotected Will Be Stolen.
3. Anything You Fail To Recognize Will Exit Your Life.
4. Asking Is The Only Evidence of Real Faith.
5. Asking Is The Proof of Humility.
6. Asking Is The Seed For Receiving.
7. Battle Is The Seed For Territorial Order And Possession.
8. Change Is Always Proportionate To Knowledge.
9. Conversations Are The Birthplace For Seasons.
10. Conversations Schedule Seasons.
11. Deception Is The Birthplace For All Pain.
12. Diligence Is Immediate Attention To An Instruction; Delayed Obedience Is The Proof of Dishonor.
13. Every Blessing Has A Cause.
14. Every Life-Battle Is A Mind-Battle.
15. Every Loss Is The Seed For Restoration.
16. Every Problem Is Always A Wisdom Problem.
17. Every Problem Is An Invitation To A Relationship.
18. Every Seed Has A Different Future.
19. Every Sin Is A Sin of Dishonor.
20. Everything You Want Is...Somewhere.
21. Giants Are Not Signs of Your Exit From Egypt; Giants Are Proofs of Your Entry Into Canaan.
22. Go Where You Are Celebrated Instead of Where You Are Tolerated.
23. Gratitude Is The Seed...For More.
24. Honor Grows In Every Environment...In Every Single Season of Your Life.
25. Honor Is The Seed For Access Into Any Environment In Every Season.

26. Honor Is The Seed...For Access.
27. Honor Is The Willingness To Magnify Difference Instead of Weakness.
28. Honor Is The Willingness To Reward Someone For Their Difference.
29. Humility Is Recognition of What You Do Not Have.
30. If You Can Understand A God-Instruction, It Was Not A God-Instruction.
31. Joseph Did Not Have A Future Until The King Had A Problem.
32. Joseph Only Needed Favor From Just One Person.
33. Knowledge Is The Seed For Change.
34. Mercy Is The Seed...For Change.
35. My Reaction To A Man of God Determines God's Reaction To Me.
36. One Day of Favor Is Worth A Thousand Days of Labor.
37. Parasites Want What Is In Your Hand; Protégés Want What Is In Your Heart.
38. Ruth Only Needed Favor From One Man To Change Her World.
39. Something I Have Been Given Will Unlock Anything I Have Been Promised.
40. Something In Your Hand Controls Your Future.
41. Something Within You Cannot Be Found In Another.
42. Something You Are Not Seeing Is Costing You.
43. Something You Have Been Given Will Create Anything Else You Have Been Promised.
44. Something You Need May Be Hidden In Someone You Do Not Enjoy.
45. The First Clue To Dishonor Is The Willingness To Ask For Something You Are Unwilling To Earn.
46. The Fragrance of Honor Is As Distinctive As The Odor of Dishonor.
47. The Law of The Seed Simply Means Something

You Have Been Given Will Create Anything Else You Have Been Promised.

48. The Proof of Humility Is The Willingness To Ask Questions.
49. The Timing of Warfare...Reveals The Importance of An Approaching Event.
50. There Are Two Ways To Get Wisdom: Mistakes And Mentors.
51. What You Keep Is Your Harvest; What You Sow Is Your Seed.
52. Whatever You Are You Reproduce.
53. When God Wants To Bless You, He Brings A Person Into Your Life.
54. Wisdom Is The Ability To Recognize Difference.
55. Words Are The Seeds...For Change.
56. Words Are The Seeds...For Feelings.
57. You Are One Seed Away From Everything You Want.
58. You Are One Seed Away From Something You Have Been Passionately Pursuing.
59. You Must Sow Up For The Blessing To Come Down.
60. You Will Always Act Like The Person You Think You Are.
61. Your Assignment Is Always The Problem God Has Assigned You To Solve For Others.
62. Your Difference Creates Your Rewards.
63. Your Difference Decides Your Importance.
64. Your Ignorance Is The Only Weapon Satan Possesses.
65. Your Memory Replays The Past; Your Imagination Preplays Your Future.
66. Your Seed Can Go Where You Cannot Go.
67. Your Self-Portrait Determines Your Self-Conduct.
68. Your Similarity Creates Your Comfort.

DECISION

Will You Accept Jesus As Your Personal Savior Today?

The Bible says, "That if thou shalt confess with thy mouth the Lord Jesus, and shalt believe in thine heart that God hath raised Him from the dead, thou shalt be saved," (Romans 10:9).

Pray this prayer from your heart today!

"Dear Jesus, I believe that You died for me and rose again on the third day. I confess I am a sinner...I need Your love and forgiveness...Come into my heart. Forgive my sins. I receive Your eternal life. Confirm Your love by giving me peace, joy and supernatural love for others. Amen."

DR. MIKE MURDOCK

is in tremendous demand as one of the most dynamic speakers in America today.

More than 17,000 audiences in over 100 countries have attended his Schools of Wisdom and conferences. Hundreds of invitations come to him from churches, colleges and business corporations. He is a noted author of over 250 books, including the best sellers, *The Leadership Secrets of Jesus* and *Secrets of the Richest Man Who Ever Lived.* Thousands view his weekly television program, *Wisdom Keys with Mike Murdock.* Many attend his Schools of Wisdom that he hosts in many cities of America.

☐ Yes, Mike, I made a decision to accept Christ as my personal Savior today. Please send me my free gift of your book, *31 Keys to a New Beginning* to help me with my new life in Christ.

CLIP AND MAIL

NAME   BIRTHDAY

ADDRESS

CITY   STATE   ZIP

PHONE   EMAIL   DFC
Mail to: **The Wisdom Center** · 4051 Denton Hwy. · Ft. Worth, TX 76117
1-817-759-BOOK · 1-817-759-2665 · 1-817-759-0300
You Will Love Our Website..! WisdomOnline.com

62

DR. MIKE MURDOCK

1 Has embraced his Assignment to Pursue...Proclaim...and Publish the Wisdom of God to help people achieve their dreams and goals.

2 Preached his first public sermon at the age of 8.

3 Preached his first evangelistic crusade at the age of 15.

4 Began full-time evangelism at the age of 19, which has continued since 1966.

5 Has traveled and spoken to more than 17,000 audiences in over 100 countries, including East and West Africa, Asia, Europe and South America.

6 Noted author of over 250 books, including best sellers, *Wisdom for Winning, Dream Seeds, The Double Diamond Principle, The Law of Recognition* and *The Holy Spirit Handbook.*

7 Created the popular *Topical Bible* series for Businessmen, Mothers, Fathers, Teenagers; *The One-Minute Pocket Bible* series, and *The Uncommon Life* series.

8 The Creator of The Master 7 Mentorship System, an Achievement Program for Believers.

9 Has composed thousands of songs such as "I Am Blessed," "You Can Make It," "God Rides On Wings of Love" and "Jesus, Just The Mention of Your Name," recorded by many gospel artists.

10 Is the Founder and Senior Pastor of The Wisdom Center, in Fort Worth, Texas...a Church with International Ministry around the world.

11 Host of *Wisdom Keys with Mike Murdock,* a weekly TV Program seen internationally.

12 Has appeared often on TBN, CBN, BET, Daystar, Inspirational Network, LeSea Broadcasting and other television network programs.

13 Has led over 3,000 to accept the call into full-time ministry.

THE MINISTRY

1 **Wisdom Books & Literature** - Over 250 best-selling Wisdom Books and 70 Teaching Tape Series.

2 **Church Crusades** - Multitudes are ministered to in crusades and seminars throughout America in "The Uncommon Wisdom Conferences." Known as a man who loves pastors, he has focused on church crusades for over 43 years.

3 **Music Ministry** - Millions have been blessed by the anointed songwriting and singing of Mike Murdock, who has made over 15 music albums and CDs available.

4 **Television** - *Wisdom Keys with Mike Murdock,* a nationally-syndicated weekly television program.

5 **The Wisdom Center** - The Church and Ministry Offices where Dr. Murdock speaks weekly on Wisdom for The Uncommon Life.

6 **Schools of The Holy Spirit** - Mike Murdock hosts Schools of The Holy Spirit in many churches to mentor believers on the Person and Companionship of The Holy Spirit.

7 **Schools of Wisdom** - In many major cities Mike Murdock hosts Schools of Wisdom for those who want personalized and advanced training for achieving "The Uncommon Dream."

8 **Missions Outreach** - Dr. Mike Murdock's overseas outreaches to over 100 countries have included crusades in East and West Africa, Asia, Europe and South America.

CPSIA information can be obtained
at www.ICGtesting.com
Printed in the USA
LVOW03s1917140617
538122LV00033B/909/P